FAITH

RESPECT YOUR TONGUE.

- ❏ When God wanted to create the world... He *spoke*.
- ❏ Words are creative forces that *bring* into existence that which never existed before.
- ❏ Your tongue is one of the greatest *gifts* placed at your command by God. Use it *wisely* and you will discover the golden key to life.

WISDOM FROM THE WORD

"Behold also the ships, which though they be so great, and are driven of fierce winds, yet are they turned about with a very small helm, whithersoever the governor listeth. Even so the tongue is a little member, and boasteth great things. Behold, how great a matter a little fire kindleth!"
James 3:4, 5

FAITH-TALK

DAY 2

SAY WHAT GOD WANTS TO HEAR.

- ❏ Your words *affect* God. Your prayers *ignite* God.

- ❏ Jesus taught His disciples *how* to pray... for provision, protection and pardon (Matthew 6:9-13).

- ❏ *Faith-Talk* is what God responds to favorably. Confess your sins...your desire for forgiveness... AND the things you need God to do in your life.

WISDOM FROM THE WORD

"If my people, which are called by my name, shall humble themselves, and pray, and seek my face, and turn from their wicked ways; then will I hear from heaven, and will forgive their sin, and will heal their land."
II Chronicles 7:14

FAITH-TALK

DAY 3

TALK TO YOURSELF.

- *External* communication is what you say to *others*. *Internal* communication is what you say to *yourself*.

- Others may *not* talk the Good Report to you... so talk it to yourself!

- What you say--about your enemy, your future, your expectations -- *affects what you believe.*

WISDOM FROM THE WORD

"This book of the law shall not depart out of thy mouth; but thou shalt meditate therein day and night, that thou mayest observe to do according to all that is written therein: for then thou shalt make thy way prosperous, and then thou shalt have good success."
Joshua 1:8

FAITH-TALK

DAY 4

TALK EXPECTATIONS NOT EXPERIENCES.

- ❏ Do not drag yesterday into your future.

- ❏ Perhaps you have just been *fired* from your job. Do not major on your feelings of rejection. Instead, point out the possibility of promotion and changes of freedom that suddenly may emerge.

- ❏ Nurture the Photograph of Possibilities within your heart. Elijah gave the widow of Zarephath a picture of her potential. It stirred her expectations of a miracle harvest in her life (I Kings 17).

WISDOM FROM THE WORD

"And let us not be weary in well doing: for in due season we shall reap, if we faint not."
Galatians 6:9

… F A I T H - T A L K

DAY 5

ABSORB THE PROMISES OF GOD.

- ❏ Study the Covenant God established with those who walk in obedience to Him.

- ❏ You can only operate in faith according to your knowledge of His will or desire for your life. For example, if you do not know that God has already provided for your healing, how can you believe Him for a miracle in your health?

- ❏ You must have a clear photograph of the will of God so your faith can implement it.

WISDOM FROM THE WORD

"...He that cometh to God must believe that He is, and that He is a rewarder of them that diligently seek Him."
Hebrews 11:6b

FAITH-TALK

DAY 6

PICTURE YOUR DESIRED FUTURE.

- ❑ Abraham had a picture of many generations of children he wanted (Genesis 17).

- ❑ Joseph had a dream of himself as a leader and he remembered it (Genesis 37).

- ❑ Know God's dream for your life. Get The Picture. Big. *BIGGER.* Fill up your mind, heart and life with it. Now make that vision consume your life... every conversation... every thought... everything around you.

WISDOM FROM THE WORD

"Where there is no vision, the people perish: but he that keepeth the law, happy is he."
Proverbs 29:18

FAITH-TALK

DAY 7

FIND FAITH FOOD.

- ❏ What you *read* affects what you believe.

- ❏ When you feed the Scriptures into your spirit man, faith comes alive and becomes a living force within you.

- ❏ Read the Bible. Read books that stir your faith in God. Nurture the Seed of Faith inside you. Acorns become oak trees.

WISDOM FROM THE WORD

"So then faith cometh by hearing, and hearing by the word of God."
Romans 10:17

FAITH-TALK

DAY 8

LISTEN TO MENTORS OF FAITH.

- ❏ Joshua learned under Moses. Timothy learned under Paul. Elisha learned under Elijah.

- ❏ Observe successful lives carefully. Secrets will surface. Reasons for success will emerge.

- ❏ Read biographies of extraordinary people who tapped into the Fountain of Faith. Their lives will excite you to new heights of faith.

WISDOM FROM THE WORD

"Wherefore seeing we also are compassed about with so great a cloud of witnesses, let us lay aside every weight, and the sin which doth so easily beset us, and let us run with patience the race that is set before us."
Hebrews 12:1

FAITH-TALK

DAY 9

REFLECT ON THE VICTORIES OF BIBLE CHAMPIONS.

- ❏ David, with a simple slingshot, killed Goliath and eventually became king (I Samuel 17).

- ❏ Joseph overcame the hatred of his brothers, false accusation and became second in power to Pharaoh (Genesis 37-41).

- ❏ Ponder and meditate on the lives of such champions... it will unleash energy, enthusiasm and faith.

WISDOM FROM THE WORD

"...The people that do know their God shall be strong, and do exploits."
Daniel 11:32b

FAITH-TALK

DAY 10

LOOSEN UP AND LAUGH.

- ❏ You are being observed today. Satan is watching to see if his tactics are working.

- ❏ *Laugh* aloud and rejoice that your circumstances are attracting the attention of God, too.

- ❏ Miracles are always birthed when things seem their worst. Satan is sensitive and very capable of being discouraged. So... make the effort to rejoice.

WISDOM FROM THE WORD

"A merry heart doeth good like a medicine: but a broken spirit drieth the bones."
Proverbs 17:22

FAITH-TALK

DAY 11

REPLAY SUCCESSES IN YOUR MIND.

- ❑ Think about *your* past battles and struggles.

- ❑ David *remembered* and *replayed* his victories over the bear and lion... *before* he ran toward Goliath (I Samuel 17:37).

- ❑ Yesterday is your history of successes. *Remember* them. *Talk* about them. Satan is the only one you will irritate!

WISDOM FROM THE WORD

"...Joshua said... take you up every man... a stone upon his shoulder... That this may be a sign... that when your children ask... What mean ye by these stones? Then ye shall answer them, That the waters of Jordan were cut off before the ark of the covenant...and these stones shall be for a memorial unto the children of Israel for ever."
Joshua 4:5-7

FAITH-TALK

DAY 12

KEEP A JOURNAL OF MIRACLES.

- ❑ God instructed Israel to pile stones to *remind their children* of the greatness of God (Joshua 4:4-10).

- ❑ Look for miracles every day... unexpected, unplanned introductions to people; information that suddenly emerges; an invitation that opens great doors of opportunities.

- ❑ *Document* these experiences *daily*. Your written journal is your private *reservoir of memories* that feed your faith.

WISDOM FROM THE WORD

"...The Lord said unto Moses, Write this for a memorial in a book, and rehearse it in the ears of Joshua..."
Exodus 17:14a

FAITH-TALK

DAY 13

MAKE IT A POINT TO BE THANKFUL.

- ❑ Thankfulness produces *joy*.

- ❑ It does not take a genius to locate, discern and detect flaws. However, it takes great awareness to see the *good* things of life.

- ❑ *Savor* God's everyday blessings. Your eyesight, your hearing, your ability to speak... and the thousands of things to be happy about.

WISDOM FROM THE WORD

"...For the joy of the Lord is your strength."
Nehemiah 8:10b

"...When they knew God, they glorified Him not as God, neither were thankful; but became vain in their imaginations, and their foolish heart was darkened."
Romans 1:21

FAITH-TALK

DAY 14

SAVOR EACH MOMENT.

- Savor means to *taste*, *feel* and *extract* all the pleasure and benefit... of each moment.

- Someone has well said, "You are going to be on the journey longer than you will be at the destination... so, enjoy the journey."

- *Always be where you are.* Do not permit your mind to race miles ahead of where your body is. Taste *NOW*... it is the future you have been talking about your entire life.

WISDOM FROM THE WORD

"...*NOW is the accepted time; behold, now is the day of salvation.*"
II Corinthians 6:2b

FAITH-TALK

DAY 15

TURN LITTLE BLESSINGS INTO CELEBRATIONS.

- ❏ Gorgeous sunsets. Laughter of children. Hot bubble baths. Vacant parking space at the mall. *Celebrate each little blessing.*

- ❏ Life is a *journey*. Focus on all the little things that make it pleasureable. Do not take today for granted.

- ❏ You have *already* received…and received… and received so much from God. *Talk it up!*

WISDOM FROM THE WORD

"Giving thanks always for all things unto God and the Father in the name of our Lord Jesus Christ."
Ephesians 5:20

FAITH-TALK

DAY 16

MAKE TODAY A MAJOR EVENT IN YOUR LIFE.

- ❏ Do not be passive today. You are ALIVE! *Act* like it!! *Talk* like it!! *Celebrate* yourself!!

- ❏ Speak a little *louder* today. Speak a little *faster*.

- ❏ Smile *bigger*... laugh *aloud*... and exude the joy of Jesus as you spread it generously over every single hour today.

WISDOM FROM THE WORD

"This is the day which the Lord hath made; we will rejoice and be glad in it."
Psalms 118:24

FAITH-TALK

DAY 17

POUR THE WORD OVER YOUR MIND DAILY.

- ❏ Your mind gathers the dirt, grime and dust of human opinion every day.

- ❏ Renew your mind to the TRUTH-- God's Word. Schedule an appointment with the Bible *daily*. The *renewing* of your mind is the key to *changes* within you.

- ❏ The Words of God are like waterfalls... *washing* and purifying your mind.

WISDOM FROM THE WORD

"That he might sanctify and cleanse it with the washing of water by the word,"
Ephesians 5:26

FAITH-TALK

DAY 18

PUT FAITH SIGNS IN YOUR HOUSE.

- ❏ What you see determines what you *feel*.
- ❏ So, put little signs on your refrigerator, bathroom mirror and bulletin boards to *stir your faith*.
- ❏ God instructed the Children of Israel to put up His Word as signs before their eyes on the door posts of their homes (Deuteronomy 11:18-25).

WISDOM FROM THE WORD

"Mine eye affecteth mine heart..."
Lamentations 3:51b

"Therefore shall ye lay up these my words in your heart...and bind them for a sign upon your hand, And thou shalt write them upon the door posts of their house..."
Deuteronomy 11:18, 20

FAITH-TALK

DAY 19

LOOK ON THE BRIGHT SIDE OF A PROBLEM.

- ❏ Learn to make lemonade out of every *lemon experience*.

- ❏ When my plane is delayed, I think of it as an extra hour to *read or catch up on correspondence*.

- ❏ Think... about all the *potential advantages* a problem might produce.

WISDOM FROM THE WORD

"Finally, brethren, whatsoever things are true, whatsoever things are honest, whatsoever things are just, whatsoever things are pure, whatsoever things are lovely, whatsoever things are of good report; if there be any virtue, and if there be any praise, think on these things."
Philippians 4:8

FAITH-TALK

DAY 20

FOCUS ON THE REWARDS OF FINISHING A TASK.

- ❏ Every task has an unpleasant side... but you must cultivate focus on the *end results* you are producing.

- ❏ Complaining people focus on the *wrong* things... their effort, toil or responsibility.

- ❏ Champions talk faith because their *focus* is on the *finished results*.

WISDOM FROM THE WORD

"...He that endureth to the end shall be saved."
Matthew 10:22b

FAITH-TALK

DAY 21

ASK A DIFFERENT QUESTION.

- Stop asking yourself questions that do not have answers such as, *"WHY did this happen to me?"* Or, *"WHY do they treat me this way?"*

- Ask yourself creative questions such as, *"WHAT can I do immediately to create changes?"* Or, *"HOW can I improve the situation?"*

- Your mind will struggle to produce answers to every question you ask it. So do not exhaust it. Ask the *right* questions.

WISDOM FROM THE WORD

"Ask, and it shall be given you; seek, and ye shall find; knock, and it shall be opened unto you:"
Matthew 7:7

FAITH-TALK

DAY 22

REFUSE THE ROLE OF THE VICTIM.

- ❏ The Victim Vocabulary includes, "I do not have an education," "I was abused in my childhood," and "My father deserted my mother..."

- ❏ Do not adopt this attitude. Fight it. *Yesterday is over.* Act like it.

- ❏ You have the anointing of God wrapped around you. You are not a captive, but a *Deliverer*. You are not a victim, but a *Victor*.

WISDOM FROM THE WORD

"Ye are of God, little children, and have overcome them: because greater is he that is in you, than he that is in the world."
I John 4:4

FAITH-TALK

DAY 23

ASSESS YOUR ATMOSPHERE.

- ❑ Indians used to wet their fingers and hold them in the wind to discern the direction of air currents.

- ❑ So you must learn to observe and *diagnose* the currents, climate and emotional atmosphere others are creating around you.

- ❑ Their words are poison or power. Their words are destructive or creative. Their words are doubt or faith building. Assess them *accurately*.

WISDOM FROM THE WORD

"And when Jesus came... He said unto them, Give place: for the maid is not dead, but sleepeth. And they laughed him to scorn. But when the people were put forth, He went in, and took her by the hand, and the maid arose." Matthew 9:23-25

FAITH-TALK

DAY 24

PINPOINT YOUR SUPPORT SYSTEM.

- ❏ Nobody succeeds alone. *Nobody*.

- ❏ Friends differ. Some *correct* you. Others *direct* you. Some make you *think*. Others make you *feel*.

- ❏ Pinpoint those who truly stimulate you... educate you... placate you. Meticulously build your foundation for friendship... a support system that is the result of *thought* instead of chance.

WISDOM FROM THE WORD

*"Two are better than one...
For if they fall, the one will lift up his fellow: but woe to him that is alone when he falleth; for he hath not another to help him up."*
Ecclesiastes 4:9, 10

FAITH-TALK

DAY 25

SCREEN DOUBTERS.

- ❏ Screen doors prevent obnoxious insects from entering your home.
- ❏ You must assertively screen out people who are *carriers* of the virus of doubt and unbelief.
- ❏ Boldly protect your ears and life from absorbing talk that does not edify and build.

WISDOM FROM THE WORD

"But he turned, and said unto Peter, Get thee behind me, Satan: thou art an offense unto me: for thou savourest not the things that be of God, but those that be of men."
Matthew 16:23

"A little leaven leaveneth the whole lump."
Galatians 5:9

FAITH-TALK

DAY 26

RECOGNIZE DOUBT PRODUCES TRAGEDIES.

- ❏ God has *feelings*. Some words grieve His heart. Some words excite His heart. Unbelief brings God great pain. Faith brings Him great pleasure.

- ❏ Twelve spies analyzed Canaan for 40 days. Moses and the people accepted the Report of Doubt from the 10 spies instead of the Report of Faith from Joshua and Caleb (Numbers 13).

- ❏ *Each day of doubt brought 365 days of heartache. Doubt is as contagious as faith.*

WISDOM FROM THE WORD

"After the number of the days in which ye searched the land, even forty days, each day for a year, shall ye bear your iniquities, even forty years, and ye shall know my breach of promise."
Numbers 14:34

FAITH-TALK

DAY 27

MARK CONTENTIOUS PEOPLE.

- ☐ *Note* those who always create conflict, complain and are hostile toward everything.

- ☐ Do not give them an opportunity to air their grievances and inject their poison into the conversation.

- ☐ *Take charge.*

WISDOM FROM THE WORD

"...Mark them which cause divisions and offences contrary to the doctrine which ye have learned; and avoid them."
Romans 16:17

"Cast out the scorner, and contention shall go out; yea, strife and reproach shall cease."
Proverbs 22:10

FAITH-TALK

DAY 28

DO NOT FEED AN ARGUMENTATIVE ATTITUDE.

- ❏ You will be challenged today. Someone will be wanting to start an argument, a quarrel.

- ❏ Do not fall for it. *Refuse* to feed a contentious spirit. It erodes your keenness and *breaks your focus.*

- ❏ *Re-direct the conversation* to the power of God, and the potential miracle about to be birthed!

WISDOM FROM THE WORD

"A soft answer turneth away wrath: but grievous words stir up anger."
Proverbs 15:1

FAITH-TALK

DAY 29

IDENTIFY COMPLAINERS.

- ❏ You will hear a lot of garbage and unbelief dumped into your ears today. *Name it for what it is.*

- ❏ Discern complainers. Recognize the spirit of murmuring that has entered someone, poisoning every conversation.

- ❏ *Do not participate.* Take the conversation upward by stating, "What an opportunity for God to perform a miracle!"

WISDOM FROM THE WORD

"...When the people complained, it displeased the Lord: and the Lord heard it; and His anger was kindled; and the fire of the Lord burnt among them, and consumed them that were in the uttermost parts of the camp."
Numbers 11:1

FAITH-TALK

DAY 30

LEARN TO LINGER IN THE PRESENCE OF GOD.

- ❏ Those who surround you influence what you become.

- ❏ Something happens in the presence of God that does not happen anywhere else. *Commands* take a moment. *Plans* take time. Linger long enough to *hear His plans*.

- ❏ Your views will change *in His presence*. Your perceptions are corrected *in His presence*. Your faith explodes *in His presence*.

WISDOM FROM THE WORD

"Thou wilt shew me the path of life: in Thy presence is fullness of joy; at Thy right hand there are pleasures for evermore."
Psalms 16:11

FAITH-TALK

DAY 31

MAKE YOURSELF UNFORGETTABLE TO GOD.

- ❏ Conversations *reveal*. What you love, hate, crave or despise is exposed by your words.

- ❏ Faith is confidence in God.

- ❏ When you speak confidently of God's integrity, and victoriously exude your anticipation of miracles... God is pleasured. God will remember you for the pleasure you created.

WISDOM FROM THE WORD

"But without faith it is impossible to please Him..."
Hebrews 11:6a

Decision Page

Will You Accept Jesus As Savior Of Your Life Today?

The Bible says, "That if thou shalt confess with thy mouth the Lord Jesus, and shall believe in thine heart that God hath raised Him from the dead, thou shalt be saved. For with the heart man believeth unto righteousness; and with the mouth confession is made unto salvation."(Rom. 10:9-10)

To receive Jesus Christ as Lord and Savior of your life, please pray this prayer from your heart today!

"Dear Jesus, I believe that you died for me and rose again on the third day. I confess I am a sinner. I need Your love and forgiveness. Come into my life, forgive my sins, and give me eternal life. I confess You now as my Lord. Thank You for my salvation, Your peace and joy. Amen."

Return This Today!

❏ Yes, Mike! I made a decision to accept Christ as my personal Savior today. Please send me my free gift copy of your book "31 Keys To A New Beginning" to help me with my new life in Christ. (B48)

"Sow A Seed Of Wisdom Into The Lives Of Those You Love!"

Here is your opportunity to invest in the lives of your Love Circle. Purchase 2 copies of *Seeds of Wisdom On Faith-Talk* for only $5 for 2 special people in your life. These dynamic daily devotionals are your answer to the "Daily Bread" of the Wisdom of God.

❏ Yes, Mike, I want to Sow 2 *Seeds of Wisdom On Faith-Talk* into 2 people that I love. I have enclosed $5 for the 2 books. Please rush them immediately. (SOW128)

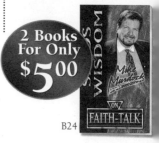

B24

Send A Self-Addressed Envelope With Check Or Money Order To: Mike Murdock
P.O. Box 99 • Dallas, TX • 75221